Joy to the World

DAILY READINGS FOR ADVENT

JOHN PIPER

Table of Contents

Preface

Advent is for adoring Jesus. At least that's our angle on it at Desiring God.

Advent is an annual season of patient waiting, hopeful expectation, soul-searching, and calendar-watching marked by many churches, Christian families, and individual followers of Jesus. There's no biblical mandate to observe Advent. It's an optional thing—a tradition that developed over the course of the church's history as a time of preparation for Christmas Day. Many of us find observing Advent to be personally enjoyable and spiritually profitable.

The English word "Advent" is from the Latin adventus, which means "coming." The advent primarily in view each December is the first coming of Jesus two millennia ago. But Jesus' second coming gets drawn in as well, as the popular Christmas carol "Joy to the World" makes plain:

> *No more let sins and sorrows grow,*
> *Nor thorns infest the ground;*
> *He comes to make His blessings flow*
> *Far as the curse is found.*

Advent begins the fourth Sunday before Christmas and ends Christmas Eve. This means that, depending on where that Sunday falls, it can be as early as November 27 or as late as December 3. Whereas Lent (the season of preparation for Easter) is always 40 days, Advent ranges in length from 22 to 29 days.

Christians throughout the world have their different ways of celebrating Advent. Some light candles.

Some sing songs. Some eat candies. Some give gifts. Some hang wreaths. Many of us do all of the above. Christians have developed many good ways of extending the celebration of Jesus' coming beyond merely the short 24 hours of December 25. The incarnation of the Son of God, "for us and for our salvation," as the old creed says it, is too big a thing to appreciate in just one day. Indeed, it's something the Christian will celebrate for all eternity.

Our prayer is that this little devotional will help you keep Jesus as the center and the greatest treasure of your Advent season. The candles and candies have their place, but we want to make sure that in all the December rush and hubbub, we adore Jesus above all.

"O Come, Let Us Adore Him" is perhaps the theme song of these Advent readings. These meditations are all about adoring Christ, the Lord. In spots, you'll hear strands of "O Come, O Come, Immanuel," and in others, "Hark! The Heralds Angels Sing." And, of course, we'll have a cameo from the magi. But the figure at the center is Jesus—the baby born in Bethlehem, the God-man in swaddling clothes, laid in a manger, destined for Calvary, sent by his Father to die and rise again for his people.

The readings are drawn from the ministry of John Piper, and as always, we encourage you to access more than 30 years of Pastor John's writing and preaching at desiringGod.org. Thanks to Tony Reinke and Jonathan Parnell who helped pull these excerpts.

These devotionals correspond with the daily readings from Pastor John in the app called "Solid Joys," which is available for free download in the iTunes store. If you find short daily reflections like these to be helpful, we recommend you look at "Solid Joys" once Advent is done.

The introduction is designed to be read before the readings begin on December 1. The conclusion can be read as an additional selection on Christmas Day (or any time before, especially if you're curious about Pastor John's favorite Christmas text). The appendix on Old Testament shadows and the coming of Christ coordinates with the meditation for December 12 (and you'll find a note in italics there).

May God be pleased to deepen and sweeten your adoring of Jesus this Advent.

David Mathis
Executive Editor
Desiring God

INTRODUCTION
What does Jesus Want this Christmas?

Father, I desire that they also, whom you have given me, may be with me where I am, to see my glory that you have given me because you loved me before the foundation of the world.

—John 17:24

What does Jesus want this Christmas? What does he ask God for?

We can find the answer in his prayers, especially his longest prayer, which is found in John 17. The climax of his desire is in verse 24.

Among all the undeserving sinners in the world, God has "given" some to Jesus. These are those whom God has drawn to the Son (John 6:44, 65). We call them *Christians*—people who have "received" Jesus as the crucified and risen Savior and Lord and Treasure of their lives (John 1:12; 3:17; 6:35; 10:11, 17-18; 20:28).

And Jesus says he wants these people to be with him. There is a common misconception that this is an expression of God's need for us, as though he were lonely. But this erroneous belief is easily debunked by the rest of the verse. Why does Jesus want us to be with him?

. . . to see my glory that you [Father] have given me because you loved me before the foundation of the world.

Jesus is not lonely. He and the Father and the Spirit are profoundly satisfied in the fellowship of the Trinity. Rather, Jesus' prayer expresses his concern for the satisfaction of *our* longing. We, not he, are starving for something. What Jesus wants for Christmas is for us to experience what we were made for—seeing and savoring his glory. Oh, that God would make this sink into our souls! Jesus made us (John 1:3) to see his glory, to really see it in all its brilliance so that we will savor it, relish it, delight in it, treasure it, and love it.

But that is only half of what Jesus wants in these final, climactic verses of his prayer. The end of the prayer (verse 26) says:

> *I made known to them your name, and I will continue to make it known, that the love with which you have loved me may be in them, and I in them.*

Jesus' final goal for us is not that we simply see his glory, but that we love him with the same love that the Father has for him.

This isn't merely an imitation of the love of the Father for the Son. When we really see Jesus' glory, the Father's very love becomes our love for the Son. We appropriate the Father's love for the Son. The Spirit bestows in our lives love for the Son by the Father.

What Jesus wants most for Christmas is that his elect be gathered in and receive what they want most—the capacity to see his glory and then savor it with the very savoring as the Father has for the Son.

What I wish most for Christmas this year is to join you (and many others) in seeing Christ in all his fullness. I want for us to be able to love what we see with a love far beyond our own half-hearted human capacities. This is our goal in these Advent devotionals: to see and savor this Jesus whose first "advent" (coming) we celebrate, and whose second advent we anticipate.

Jesus prays for us this Christmas. "Father, show them my glory and give them the very delight in me that you have in me." Oh, may we see Christ with the eyes of God and savor Christ with the heart of God. That is the Good News of Great Joy, the gift Christ came to purchase for sinners at the cost of his death in our place.

DECEMBER 1
Prepare the Way

He will turn many of the children of Israel to the Lord their God, and he will go before him in the spirit and power of Elijah, to turn the hearts of the fathers to the children, and the disobedient to the wisdom of the just, to make ready for the Lord a people prepared.

—Luke 1:16-17

What John the Baptist did for Israel, Advent can do for us. Don't let Christmas find you unprepared—I mean, spiritually unprepared. Its joy and impact will be so much greater if you are ready!

Here are some ways to prepare your heart for Advent:

First, meditate on the fact that you need a Savior.

Christmas is an indictment before it becomes a delight. It will not have its intended effect until you feel your need for a Savior desperately. Let these short Advent meditations help awaken in you a bittersweet sense of your need for the Savior.

Second, engage in sober self-examination. Advent is to Christmas what Lent is to Easter. "Search me, O God, and know my heart! Try me and know my thoughts! And see if there be any grievous way in me, and lead me in the way everlasting!" (Psalm 139:23–24). Let every heart prepare him room . . . by cleaning house.

Third, build God-centered anticipation, expectancy, and excitement into your home—especially for the children in it. If you are excited about Christ, they will be too. If you can only make Christmas exciting with material things, how will children get a thirst for God? Bend the efforts of your imagination to make the wonder of the King's arrival visible for children.

Fourth, be much in the Scriptures and memorize the great passages. "Is not my word like fire, declares the LORD" (Jeremiah 23:29)? Gather 'round that fire this Advent season. It is warm. It is sparkling with the many-hued colors of grace. It is healing for a thousand hurts and light for dark nights.

DECEMBER 2
Mary's Magnificent God

*My soul magnifies the Lord, and my spirit rejoices
in God my Savior, for he has looked on the humble
estate of his servant. For behold, from now on all gen-
erations will call me blessed; for he who is mighty has
done great things for me, and holy is his name. And
his mercy is for those who fear him from generation
to generation. He has shown strength with his arm; he
has scattered the proud in the thoughts of their hearts;
he has brought down the mighty from their thrones
and exalted those of humble estate; he has filled the
hungry with good things, and the rich he has sent
away empty. He has helped his servant Israel, in re-
membrance of his mercy, as he spoke to our fathers,
to Abraham and to his offspring forever.*

—Luke 1:46-55

Mary sees clearly the most remarkable thing
about God: He is about to change the course of
all human history. The most important three decades
in all of time are about to begin.

And where is God at this crucial moment? Sur-
prisingly, he is occupying himself with two obscure,
humble women—one old and barren (Elizabeth), one
young and virginal (Mary). When the angel appears,
Mary is so moved by this vision of God, the lover of
the lowly, that she breaks out in song—a song that has
come to be known as "the Magnificat" (Luke 1:46-55).

Mary and Elizabeth are wonderful heroines in
Luke's account. He loves the faith of these women.
The thing that impresses him most, it appears, and
the thing he wants to impress on Theophilus, his no-

ble reader, is the lowliness and cheerful humility of Elizabeth and Mary.

Elizabeth says, "Why is this granted to me that the mother of my Lord should come to me?" (Luke 1:43). And Mary says, "He has looked on the humble estate of his servant" (Luke 1:48).

The only people whose souls can truly magnify the Lord are people like Elizabeth and Mary—people who acknowledge their lowly estate and are overwhelmed by the condescension of the magnificent God.

DECEMBER 3
The Long-Awaited Visitation

*Blessed be the Lord God of Israel, for he has visited
and redeemed his people and has raised up a horn
of salvation for us in the house of his servant David,
as he spoke by the mouth of his holy prophets from
of old, that we should be saved from our enemies
and from the hand of all who hate us.*

—Luke 1:68–71

Notice two remarkable things from these words of Zechariah in Luke 1.

First, note Zechariah's faith. Nine months earlier, Zechariah could not believe his wife would have a child. Now, filled with the Holy Spirit, he is so confident of God's redeeming work in the coming Messiah that he puts it in the past tense. Zechariah has learned to take God at his word and so has a remarkable assurance: "God has visited and redeemed!" A promised act of God is as good as done.

Second, the coming of Jesus the Messiah is a visitation of God to our world: "The God of Israel has *visited* and redeemed." For centuries, the Jewish people had languished under the conviction that God had withdrawn: the spirit of prophecy had ceased, Israel had fallen into the hands of Rome, and even the godly in Israel were growing weary in awaiting the visitation of God. Luke 2:25 tells us that the devout Simeon was "waiting for the consolation of Israel." And in Luke 2:38, the prayerful Anna was "waiting for the redemption of Jerusalem."

These were days of great expectation. Now the long-awaited visitation of God was about to happen—indeed. He was about to come in a way no one expected.

DECEMBER 4
For God's Ordinary People

In those days a decree went out from Caesar Augustus that all the world should be registered. This was the first registration when Quirinius was governor of Syria. And all went to be registered, each to his own town. And Joseph also went up from Galilee, from the town of Nazareth, to Judea, to the city of David, which is called Bethlehem, because he was of the house and lineage of David, to be registered with Mary, his betrothed, who was with child.

—Luke 2:1-5

Have you ever thought what an amazing thing it is that God ordained beforehand that the Messiah would be born in Bethlehem (as the prophecy in Micah 5 shows); and that he so ordained things that when the time came, the Messiah's mother and legal father were living in Nazareth; and that in order to fulfill his word and bring two insignificant people to Bethlehem that first Christmas, God put it in the heart of Caesar Augustus that all the Roman world should be enrolled, each in his own town?

Have you ever felt, like me, ordinary and insignificant in a world of seven billion people, where all the news is of big political and economic and social movements and of outstanding people with lots of power and prestige?

If you have, don't let that make you disheartened or unhappy. For it is implicit in Scripture that all the mammoth political forces and all the giant industrial complexes, without their even knowing it, are being guided by God, not for their own sake but for the sake of God's ordinary people—the ordinary Mary and the ordinary Joseph who have to be moved from Nazareth to Bethlehem. God wields an empire to bless his children.

Do not think, because you experience adversity, that the hand of the Lord is shortened. It is not our prosperity but our holiness that he seeks with all his heart. And to that end, he rules the whole world. As Proverbs 21:1 says, "The king's heart is a stream of water in the hand of the LORD; he turns it wherever he will."

He is a big God for ordinary people, and we have great cause to rejoice that, unbeknownst to them, all the kings and presidents and premiers and chancellors of the world follow the sovereign decrees of our Father in heaven so that we, the children, might be conformed to the image of his Son, Jesus Christ.

DECEMBER 5
No Detour from Calvary

And while they were there, the time came for her to give birth. And she gave birth to her firstborn son and wrapped him in swaddling cloths and laid him in a manger, because there was no place for them in the inn.

—Luke 2:6-7

Now, you would think that if God so rules the world as to use an empire-wide census to bring Mary and Joseph to Bethlehem, he surely could have seen to it that a room was available in the inn.

Yes, he could have. And Jesus could have been born into a wealthy family. He could have turned stones into bread in the wilderness. He could have called 10,000 angels to his aid in Gethsemane. He could have come down from the cross and saved himself. The question is not what God could do, but what he willed to do.

God's will was that though Christ was rich, yet for your sake, he became poor. The "No Vacancy" signs over all the motels in Bethlehem were for your sake. "For your sake he became poor" (2 Corinthians 8:9). God rules all things—even motel capacities—for the sake of his children. The Calvary road begins with a "No Vacancy" sign in Bethlehem and ends with the spitting and scoffing of the cross in Jerusalem.

We must not forget that he said, "If anyone would come after me, let him deny himself and take up his cross" (Matthew 16:24). We join him on the Calvary road and hear him say, "Remember the word that I said to you: 'A servant is not greater than his master.' If they persecuted me, they will also persecute you" (John 15:20).

To the one who calls out enthusiastically, "I will follow you wherever you go!" (Matthew 8:19), Jesus responds, "Foxes have holes, and birds of the air have nests, but the Son of Man has nowhere to lay his head" (Matthew 8:20).

Yes, God could have seen to it that Jesus had a room at his birth. But that would have been a detour off the Calvary road.

DECEMBER 6
Peace to Those with Whom He's Pleased

"And this will be a sign for you: you will find a baby wrapped in swaddling cloths and lying in a manger." And suddenly there was with the angel a multitude of the heavenly host praising God and saying, "Glory to God in the highest, and on earth peace among those with whom he is pleased!"

—Luke 2:12-14

There is a somber note sounded in the angels' praise. The peace is for those on whom his favor rests, among those with whom he is pleased. We know that without faith it is impossible to please God, so Christmas does not bring peace to all.

"This is the judgment:" Jesus said, "the light has come into the world, and people loved the darkness rather than the light because their works were evil" (John 3:19). Or as the aged Simeon said when he saw the child Jesus, "Behold this child is appointed for the fall and rising of many in Israel, and for a sign that is opposed . . . that thoughts from many hearts may be revealed" (Luke 2:34-35). O, how many there are who look out on a bleak and chilly Christmas Day and see no more than that.

"He came to his own, and his own people did not receive him. But to all who did receive him . . . he gave the right to become children of God." (John 1:11-12). It was only to his disciples that Jesus said, "Peace I leave with you; my peace I give to you. Not as the world gives do I give to you. Let not your hearts be troubled, neither let them be afraid" (John 14:27).

The key that unlocks the treasure chest of God's peace is faith in the promises of God. The people who enjoy the peace of God that surpasses all understanding are those who in everything by prayer and supplication let their requests be made known to God. So Paul prays, "May the God of hope fill you with all joy and peace in believing" (Romans 15:13). And when we trust the promises of God and have joy and peace and love, then God is glorified.

Glory to God in the highest, and on earth peace to men with whom he is pleased—men who would believe.

DECEMBER 7
Messiah for the Magi

Now after Jesus was born in Bethlehem of Judea in the days of Herod the king, behold, wise men from the east came to Jerusalem, saying, "Where is He who has been born king of the Jews?"

—Matthew 2:1-2

Unlike Luke, Matthew does not tell us about the shepherds coming to visit Jesus in the stable. His focus is immediately on foreigners coming from the East to worship Jesus. Here the first worshipers are court magicians or astrologers or wise men, not from Israel, but from the East—perhaps from Babylon. They were Gentiles. Unclean.

Matthew also closes his book with this same theme, showing that Jesus is the universal Messiah for all the nations, not just for Jews. The last words of Jesus are, "All authority in heaven and on earth has been given to me. Go therefore and make disciples of all nations" (Matthew 28:18-19).

This not only opened the door for the Gentiles to rejoice in the Messiah; it added proof that Jesus was the Messiah because he fulfilled the many prophecies that the nations and kings would, in fact, come to him as the ruler of the world. For example, Isaiah 60:3 says, "Nations shall come to your light, and kings to the brightness of your rising." So Matthew adds proof to the messiahship of Jesus by showing that he is a King and Promise-Fulfiller for all nations, not just Israel.

DECEMBER 8
Bethlehem's Supernatural Star

Where is he who has been born king of the Jews?
For we saw his star when it rose and have come to
worship him.

—Matthew 2:2

*O*ver and over the Bible baffles our curiosity about
how certain things happened. How did this
"star" get the magi from the East to Jerusalem? It does
not say that it led them or went before them, it only says
they saw a star in the east (verse 2) and came to Jerusalem.

And how did that star go before them in the little
five-mile walk from Jerusalem to Bethlehem, as verse 9
says it did? And how did the star stand "over the place
where the child was"? The answer is, we do not know.
There are numerous efforts to explain it in terms of
conjunctions of planets or comets or supernovas or
miraculous lights, but the truth is, we just don't know.

I want to exhort you not to become preoccupied
with developing theories that are only tentative in the
end and have very little spiritual significance. In fact, I
will risk a generalization to warn you: People who are
exercised and preoccupied with such things as how
the star worked and how the Red Sea split and how the
manna fell and how Jonah survived the fish and how
the moon turns to blood are generally people who have
what I call a mentality for the marginal. You do not see
in them a deep cherishing of the great central things of
the gospel—the holiness of God, the ugliness of sin, the
helplessness of man, the death of Christ, justification

by faith alone, the sanctifying work of the Spirit, the glory of Christ's return, and the final judgment. They always seem to be taking you down a sidetrack with a new article or book. There is little centered rejoicing.

What is plain concerning this matter of the star is that it is doing something that it cannot do on its own: it is guiding magi to the Son of God to worship him.

There is only one Person in biblical thinking who can be behind such intentionality in the stars—God himself. So the lesson is plain: God is guiding foreigners to Christ to worship him. And he is doing it by exerting global—probably even universal—influence and power.

Luke shows God influencing the entire Roman Empire so that the census comes at the exact time to get a virgin to Bethlehem to fulfill prophecy with her delivery, and Matthew shows God influencing the stars in the sky to get foreign magi to Bethlehem so that they can worship him. This is God's design. He did it then, and he is still doing it now. His aim is that the nations—all the nations (Matthew 24:14)—worship his Son. This is God's will for everybody in your office at work, in your neighborhood, and in your home.

At the beginning of Matthew we have a "come-see" pattern. But in the end, the pattern is "go-tell." The magi came and saw. We are to go and tell. In both cases, the purpose of God is the ingathering of the nations to worship his Son. The magnifying of Christ in the white-hot worship of all nations is the reason the world exists.

DECEMBER 9
Two Kinds of Opposition to Jesus

When Herod the king heard this, he was troubled, and all Jerusalem with him.

—Matthew 2:3

*J*esus is troubling to people who do not want to worship him, and this creates opposition against those who do. This is probably not the main point in the mind of Matthew, but it is inescapable as the story goes on.

There are two kinds of people who do not want to worship Jesus the Messiah. The first kind is the people who simply do nothing about Jesus. He is a nonentity in their lives. This group is represented by the chief priests and scribes: "Assembling all the chief priests and scribes of the people, [Herod] inquired of them where the Christ was to be born" (Matthew 2:4). Well, they told him, and that was that—back to business as usual. The sheer silence and inactivity of the religious leaders are overwhelming given the magnitude of what was happening.

Compare that with the reaction of Herod and the rest of Jerusalem: "When Herod the king heard this, he was troubled, and all Jerusalem with him" (verse 3). In other words, the rumor was going around that someone thought the Messiah was born, and everyone but the chief priests took note. Why did they not go with the magi? They were not interested. They did not want to worship the true God.

The second kind of people who do not want to worship Jesus are those who are deeply threatened by him. Herod was deeply afraid—so much so that he schemed and lied and then committed mass murder just to get rid of Jesus.

Still today, these two kinds of opposition will come against Christ and his worshipers: indifference and hostility. Are you in one of those groups? Let this Christmas be the time when you reconsider the Messiah and ponder what it is to worship him.

DECEMBER 10
Gold, Frankincense, and Myrrh

When they saw the star, they rejoiced exceedingly with great joy. And going into the house they saw the child with Mary his mother, and they fell down and worshiped him. Then, opening their treasures, they offered him gifts, gold and frankincense and myrrh.

—Matthew 2:10-11

The gifts of the magi were not given by way of assistance or need-meeting. God is not "served by human hands, as though he needed anything" (Acts 17:25). Indeed, it would dishonor a monarch if foreign visitors came with royal care packages. Nor were these gifts meant to be bribes. Deuteronomy 10:17 says that God takes no bribe. So what was their significance? And what do they teach us about worship?

The magi's gifts were intensifiers of desire for Christ himself in much the same way fasting is for us. When you give this type of gift to Christ, it's a way of saying, "The joy that I pursue (verse 10) is not the hope of getting rich with things from you. I have not come to you for what you might give me, but for your-self. And this desire I now intensify and demonstrate by giving up these things in the hope of enjoying you more and enjoying things less. By giving to you what you do not need, and what I might enjoy, I am saying more earnestly and more authentically, 'You are my treasure, not these things.'"

I think that's what it means to worship God with gifts of gold and frankincense and myrrh.

May God awaken in us a desire for Christ himself. May we say from the heart, "Lord Jesus, you are the Messiah, the King of Israel. All nations will come and bow down before you. God wields the world to see that you are worshiped. Therefore, whatever opposition I may find, I joyfully ascribe authority and dignity to you, and bring my gifts to say that you alone can satisfy my heart, not these."

DECEMBER 11
Why Jesus Came

*Since therefore the children share in flesh and blood,
he himself likewise partook of the same things, that
through death he might destroy the one who has the
power of death, that is, the devil, and deliver all
those who through fear of death were subject to life-
long slavery.*

—Hebrews 2:14-15

Hebrews 2:14-15 connects the beginning and the
end of Jesus' earthly life, and in so doing, makes
clear why he came. These verses would be great to
use with an unbelieving friend or family member to
take them step-by-step through your Christian view
of Christmas. It might go something like this . . .

*"Since therefore the children share in flesh and
blood . . ."*

The term "children" is taken from the previous
verse and refers to the spiritual offspring of Christ,
the Messiah (see Isaiah 8:18; 53:10). These are also
the "children of God." In sending Christ, God has
the salvation of his "children" in view. It is true that
"God so loved the world, that he gave [Jesus] (John
3:16)." But it is also true that God was especially
gathering "into one the children of God who are scattered abroad" (John 11:52). God's design was to offer
Christ to the world, and to effect the salvation of his
children—those who experience adoption into God's
family by receiving Christ (John 1:12).

*". . . he himself likewise partook of the same things
[flesh and blood] . . ."*

Christ existed before the Incarnation. He is the eternal Word. He was with God and was God (John 1:1;
Colossians 2:9). But he took on flesh and blood and
clothed his deity with humanity. He became fully
man while remaining fully God. It is a great mystery
in many ways, but it is at the heart of our faith and is
what the Bible teaches.

". . . that through death . . ."

The reason Jesus became man was to die. As God, he
could not die for sinners. But as a man he could. His
aim was to die. Therefore, he had to be born human.
Good Friday is the reason for Christmas.

*". . . he might destroy the one who has the power of
death, that is, the devil . . ."*

In dying, Christ de-fanged the devil by covering all
our sin. This means that Satan has no legitimate
grounds to accuse us before God. "Who shall bring
any charge against God's elect? It is God who justi-
fies" (Romans 8:33). On what grounds does he justi-
fy? Through the blood of Jesus (Romans 5:9).

Satan's ultimate weapon against us is our own sin.
If the death of Jesus takes it away, the chief weapon
of the devil is taken out of his hand. He cannot make

a case for our death penalty because the Judge has
acquitted us by the death of his own Son!

> *". . . and deliver all those who through fear of death
> were subject to lifelong slavery."*

We are free from the fear of death because God has
justified us. Satan cannot overturn that decree. And
God means for our ultimate safety to have an imme-
diate effect on our lives. The assured happy ending
takes away the slavery and fear of the now. If we do
not need to fear our last and greatest enemy—death—
then we do not need to fear anything. We can be free:
free for joy, free for others.

What a great Christmas present from God to us,
and from us to the world!

DECEMBER 12
Replacing the Shadows

Now the point in what we are saying is this: we have such a high priest, one who is seated at the right hand of the throne of the Majesty in heaven, a minister in the holy places, in the true tent that the Lord set up, not man.

—Hebrews 8:1-2

*T*he point of the book of Hebrews is that Jesus Christ, God's Son, has not just come to fit into the earthly system of priestly ministry as the best and final human priest, but he has come to fulfill and put an end to that system and to orient all our attention on himself ministering for us in heaven.

The Old Testament Tabernacle and priests and sacrifices were shadows. Now the reality has come, and the shadows pass away.

Here's an illustration of what this means. Suppose you are a young child, and you and your mom get separated in the grocery store. You are scared and panicked and don't know which way to go. Then you run to the end of an aisle, and just before you start to cry, you see a shadow on the floor that looks just like your mom. It makes you really happy, and you feel hope. But which is better? The happiness of seeing the shadow, or having your mom step around the corner and seeing that it's her?

That's a simple example of what Christmas means. Jesus came to be our High Priest. Christmas is the replacement of shadows with the real thing.

(For more on how the coming of Christ replaces the Old Testament, see the appendix at the end of this book.)

DECEMBER 13
The Final Reality is Here

Now the point in what we are saying is this: we have such a high priest, one who is seated at the right hand of the throne of the Majesty in heaven, a minister in the holy places, in the true tent that the Lord set up, not man.

—Hebrews 8:1-2

*J*esus, the true and final priest, stands between us and God. He is the intermediary who makes us right with God and prays for us to God. He is not an ordinary, weak, sinful, dying priest like in the Old Testament days. He is the Son of God—strong, sinless, with an indestructible life.

Not only that, he does not minister in an earthly Tabernacle, with all its limitations of place and size and wearing out and being moth-eaten and being soaked and burned and torn and stolen. No, verse 2 says that Christ is ministering for us "in the true tent that the Lord set up, not man." This is the real thing in heaven. This is what cast its shadow on Mount Sinai when the law was given to Moses.

Furthermore, Jesus, our High Priest, is seated at the right hand of the Majesty in heaven. No Old Testament priest could ever say that.

Jesus deals directly with God, the Father. He has a place of honor beside God. He is loved and respected infinitely by God. He is constantly with God. This is not shadow reality like curtains and bowls and tables and candles and robes and tassels and sheep and goats and pigeons. This is the final, ultimate reality:

God and his Son interacting in love and holiness for our eternal salvation.

The three persons of the Godhead are in relationship, dealing with each other concerning how their majesty and holiness and love and justice and goodness and truth shall be manifested in a redeemed people.

DECEMBER 14
Making it Real for His People

Christ has obtained a ministry that is as much more excellent than the old as the covenant he mediates is better, since it is enacted on better promises.

—Hebrews 8:6

*C*hrist is the mediator of a new covenant. His blood—the blood of the covenant (Luke 22:20; Hebrews 13:20)—purchased the fulfillment of God's promises for us. And the end result is that God brings about our inner transformation by the Spirit of Christ.

God works all his transformation in us through faith in all that he is for us in Christ. The new covenant is purchased by the blood of Christ, effected by the Spirit of Christ, and appropriated by faith in Christ.

The best place to see Christ working as the mediator of the new covenant is in Hebrews 13:20-21:

Now may the God of peace who brought again from the dead our Lord Jesus, the great shepherd of the sheep, by the blood of the eternal covenant, equip you with everything good that you may do his will, working in us that which is pleasing in his sight, through Jesus Christ, to whom be glory forever and ever. Amen.

The words "working in us that which is pleasing in his sight" describe what happens when God writes the law on our hearts in the new covenant. And the words "through Jesus Christ" describe Jesus as the mediator of this glorious work of sovereign grace.

So the meaning of Christmas is not only that God replaces shadows with reality, but also that he takes the reality and makes it real to his people. He writes it on our hearts. He does not lay his Christmas gift of salvation and transformation down for you to pick up in your own strength; he picks it up and puts it in your heart and in your mind, and seals to you that you are a child of God.

DECEMBER 15
Life and Death at Christmas

The thief comes only to steal and kill and destroy. I came that they may have life and have it abundantly.

—John 10:10

*A*s I was about to begin this devotional, I received word that Marion Newstrum had just died. She and her husband, Elmer, have been part of Bethlehem longer than most of our members have been alive. Marion was 87. They had been married 64 years.

When I spoke to Elmer and asked how he was doing, he said, "Jesus has been a true friend." I pray that all Christians will be able to say at the end of life, "Christ has been a true friend."

Each Advent, I mark the anniversary of my mother's death. She was cut off in her fifty-sixth year in a bus accident in Israel. It was December 16, 1974. Those events are incredibly real to me even today. If I allow myself, I can easily come to tears over them. We buried her the day after Christmas—what a precious Christmas it was!

Many of you will feel your loss this Christmas more pointedly than before. Don't block it out. Let it come. Feel it. What is love for, if not to intensify our affections—in both life and death? But, Oh, do not be bitter! It is tragically self-destructive to be bitter.

Jesus came at Christmas that we might have eternal life. "I came that they might have life and have it abundantly" (John 10:10). Do you feel restless for home? I have family coming home for the holidays, and that feels good. I think the reason it feels good is that they and I are destined in the depths of our being for an ultimate Homecoming. All other homecomings are foretastes, and foretastes are good.

Unless they become substitutes. O, don't let all the sweet things of this season become substitutes of the final, great, all-satisfying sweetness of knowing Jesus. Let every loss and every delight send your heart a-homing after heaven.

Christmas. What is it but this: "I came that they might have life." Marion Newstrum, Ruth Piper, and you and I—that we might have life, now and forever.

Make your now the richer and deeper this Christmas by drinking at the fountain of forever. It is so near.

DECEMBER 16
God's Most Successful Setback

Therefore God has highly exalted him and bestowed on him the name that is above every name, so that at the name of Jesus every knee should bow, in heaven and on earth and under the earth, and every tongue confess that Jesus Christ is Lord, to the glory of God the Father.

—Philippians 2:9-11

Christmas was God's most successful setback. He has always delighted to show his power through apparent defeat. He makes tactical retreats in order to win strategic victories.

Consider the story of Joseph from the Old Testament. Joseph was promised glory and power in his dream (Genesis 37:5-11). But to achieve that victory, he had to become a slave in Egypt. And as if that were not enough, when his conditions improved because of his integrity, he was made worse than a slave—a prisoner.

But it was all planned by God himself. For there in prison, he met Pharaoh's butler, who eventually brought him to Pharaoh, who put him over Egypt. What an unlikely route to glory! But that is God's way—even for his Son. Jesus emptied himself and took the form of a slave. He became worse than a slave—a prisoner—and was executed. But like Joseph, Jesus kept his integrity. "Therefore God has highly exalted him and bestowed on him the name that is above every name, so that at the name of Jesus every knee should bow" (Philippians 2:9-10).

And this is God's way for us, too. We are promised glory—if we will suffer with him (Romans 8:17). The way up is down. The way forward is backward. The way to success is through divinely appointed setbacks. They will always look and feel like a failure.

But if Joseph and Jesus teach us anything this Christmas, it is this: "God meant it for good!" (Genesis 50:20).

You fearful saints fresh courage take
The clouds you so much dread
Are big with mercy and will break
In blessings on your head.

—Hymn written by **William Cowper.**

December 17
The Greatest Salvation Imaginable

Behold, the days are coming, declares the LORD, when I will make a new covenant with the house of Israel and the house of Judah . . .

—Jeremiah 31:31

God is just and holy and separated from sinners like us. This is our main problem in every season, including Christmas. How shall we get right with a just and holy God?

God is merciful, and he promised in Jeremiah 31 (five hundred years before Christ) that someday he would do something new. He would replace shadows with the reality of the Messiah. And he would powerfully move into our lives and write his will on our hearts so that we are not constrained from the outside, but are willing from the inside to love him, trust him, and follow him.

It is the greatest salvation imaginable—God offers us the greatest reality in the universe to enjoy and then moves in us so that we can enjoy it with the greatest freedom and joy possible. That is a Christmas gift worth singing about.

But there is a huge obstacle: our sin. Our unrighteousness separated us from God. How can a holy and just God treat us sinners with so much kindness as to give us the greatest reality in the universe (his Son) to enjoy with the greatest joy possible?

The answer is that God put our sins on his Son, and judged them there so that he could put them out of his mind and deal with us mercifully while remaining just and holy. Hebrews 9:28 says Christ was "offered once to bear the sins of many."

Christ bore our sins in his own body when he died. He took our judgment. He canceled our guilt. And that means our sins are gone. They do not remain in God's mind as a basis for condemnation. In that sense, he "forgets" them. They are consumed in the death of Christ.

God is now free, in his justice, to lavish us with the new covenant. He gives us Christ, the greatest reality in the universe, for our enjoyment. And he writes his own will—his own heart—on our heart so that we can love and trust and follow Christ from the inside out, with freedom and joy.

DECEMBER 18
The Christmas Model for Missions

As you sent me into the world, so I have sent them into the world.

—John 17:18

Christmas is a model for missions, and missions are a mirror of Christmas. Jesus tells us, "As I, so you."

This means that we will face danger and trouble. Christ came to his own, and his own received him not. So you. They plotted against him. So you. He had no permanent home. So you. They trumped up false charges against him. So you. They whipped and mocked him. So you. He died after three years of ministry. So you.

But there is a worse danger than any of these, which Jesus escaped. In the mid-sixteenth century, Francis Xavier (1506–1552), a Catholic missionary, wrote to Father Perez of Malacca (what is part of Indonesia today) about the perils of his mission to China. He said,

> *The danger of all dangers would be to lose trust and confidence in the mercy of God. . . . To distrust him would be a far more terrible thing than any physical evil which all the enemies of God put together could inflict on us, for without God's permission neither the devils nor their human ministers could hinder us in the slightest degree.*

The greatest danger a missionary faces is to distrust the mercy of God. If that danger is avoided, then all other dangers lose their sting. God makes every dagger a scepter in our hand. As J.W. Alexander says, "Each instant of present labor is to be graciously repaid with a million ages of glory."

Christ escaped the danger of distrust. Therefore God has highly exalted him! Remember this Advent that Christmas is a model for missions. *As I, so you.* Mission often brings danger, but the greatest danger is distrusting God's mercy. Succumb to this, and all is lost. Conquer here, and nothing can harm you for a million ages.

DECEMBER 19
Christmas is for Freedom

> *Since therefore the children share in flesh and blood,*
> *he himself likewise partook of the same things, that*
> *through death he might destroy the one who has the*
> *power of death, that is, the devil, and deliver all*
> *those who through fear of death were subject to life-*
> *long slavery.*
>
> —Hebrews 2:14-15

Jesus became man because what was needed was the death of a man who was more than man. The incarnation was God locking himself into death row.

Christ did not risk death, he embraced it. That is precisely why he came: not to be served, but to serve, and to give his life a ransom for many (Mark 10:45). No wonder Satan tried to turn Jesus from the Cross! The Cross was Satan's destruction. How did Jesus destroy him? The "power of death" is the ability to hold men in bondage through fear of death. It is the power to keep men in sin so that death comes as a horrid thing.

But Jesus stripped Satan of this power. He disarmed him. He molded a breastplate of righteousness for us that makes us immune to the devil's condemnation. By his death, Jesus wiped away all our sins. And a person without sin puts Satan out of business. His treason is aborted. His cosmic treachery is foiled. "His rage we can endure, for, lo, his doom is sure." (Hymn written by **Martin Luther**). The Cross has run him through. And he will gasp his last before long.

Christmas is for freedom—freedom from the fear of death.

Jesus took our nature in Bethlehem, to die our death in Jerusalem, that we might be fearless in our city. Yes, *fearless*. Because if the biggest threat to my joy is gone, then why should I fret over the little things? How can anyone say, "Well, I'm not afraid to die, but I'm afraid to lose my job"?

If death is no longer a fear, we're free, really free. Free to take any risk under the sun for Christ and for love. No more bondage to anxiety. If the Son has set you free, you shall be free, indeed!

DECEMBER 20
Christmas Solidarity

The reason the Son of God appeared was to destroy the works of the devil.

—1 John 3:8

*T*he assembly line of Satan turns out millions of sins every day. He packs them into huge cargo planes and flies them to heaven and spreads them out before God and laughs and laughs and laughs.

Some people work full-time on the assembly line of sin. Others have quit their jobs there and only now and then return. Every minute of work on the assembly line makes God the laughingstock of Satan. Sin is Satan's business because he hates the light and beauty and purity and glory of God. Nothing pleases him more than when creatures distrust and disobey their Maker.

But Christmas is good news for man and good news for God.

"The saying is trustworthy and deserving of full acceptance, that Christ Jesus came into the world to save sinners" (1 Timothy 1:15). That's good news for us.

"The reason the Son of God appeared was to destroy the works of the devil" (1 John 3:8). That's good news for God.

Jesus has come to lead a strike at Satan's assembly plant. He has walked right into the plant, called for the solidarity of the faithful, and begun a massive walkout. Christmas is a call to go on strike at the assembly plant of sin. No negotiations with the management. No bargaining. Just single-minded, un-swerving opposition to the product.

Christmas solidarity aims to ground the cargo planes. It will not use force or violence, but with re-lentless devotion to truth it will expose the life-de-stroying conditions of the devil's industry.

Christmas solidarity will not give up until a com-plete shutdown has been achieved. When sin has been destroyed, God's name will be wholly exonerat-ed. No one will be laughing at him anymore.

If you want to give a gift to God this Christmas, walk off Satan's assembly line and never go back. Take up your place in the picket line of love. Join Christmas solidarity until the majestic name of God is cleared and he stands glorious amid the accolades of the righteous.

DECEMBER 21
The Birth of the Ancient of Days

Then Pilate said to him, "So you are a king?" Jesus answered, "You say that I am a king. For this purpose I was born and for this purpose I have come into the world—to bear witness to the truth. Everyone who is of the truth listens to my voice."

—John 18:37

*T*his is a great Christmas text even though it comes from the end of Jesus' life on earth, rather than the beginning. The uniqueness of the birth of Christ is that he did not originate at his birth. He existed before he was born in a manger. The personhood, character, and personality of Jesus of Nazareth existed before the man Jesus of Nazareth was born.

The theological word to describe this mystery is not creation, but *Incarnation*. The person—not the body, but the essential personhood—of Jesus existed before he was born as a man. His birth was not a coming into being of a new person, but a coming into the world of an infinitely old person.

Micah 5:2 put it like this, 700 years before Jesus was born:

But you, O Bethlehem Ephrathah, who are too little to be among the clans of Judah, from you shall come forth for me one who is to be ruler in Israel, whose coming forth is from of old, from ancient days.

The mystery of the birth of Jesus is not merely that he was born of a virgin. That miracle was intended by God to witness to an even greater one—namely, that the child born at Christmas was a person who existed "from of old, from ancient days," the eternal, almighty God.

DECEMBER 22
That You May Believe

Now Jesus did many other signs in the presence of the disciples, which are not written in this book; but these are written so that you may believe that Jesus is the Christ, the Son of God, and that by believing you may have life in his name.

—John 20:30-31

*M*any of us have grown up in church and can recite the great doctrines of our faith in our sleep and often yawn through the Apostles' Creed. Something must be done to help us once more feel the awe, the fear, the astonishment, the wonder of the Son of God, begotten by the Father from all eternity, reflecting all the glory of God, being the very image of his person, through whom all things were created, upholding the universe by the word of his power.

You can read every fairy tale, every mystery thriller, every ghost story that was ever written, and you will never find anything so shocking, so strange, so weird, and so spellbinding as the story of the incarnation of the Son of God.

How dead we are! How callous and unfeeling to his glory and his story! How often have I had to repent and say, "God, I am sorry that the stories men have made up stir my emotions, my awe and wonder and admiration and joy, more than your own true story." How easily we dismiss the real living contact between us the eternal God of the universe.

When Jesus said, "For this purpose I have come into the world," he said something as crazy and weird and strange and eerie as any statement in science fiction that you have ever read (John 18:37).

O, how I pray for a breaking forth of the Spirit of God upon me and upon you. I pray for the Holy Spirit to break into my experience in a frightening way, to wake me up to the unimaginable reality of God.

One of these days lightning is going to fill the sky from the rising of the sun to its setting, and there is going to appear in the clouds one like a Son of Man with his mighty angels in flaming fire. And we will see him clearly. Whether from terror or sheer excitement, we will tremble, and we will wonder how we ever lived so long with such a domesticated, harmless Christ.

These things are written that you might believe—really believe—that Jesus Christ is the Son of God who came into the world.

DECEMBER 23
God's Indescribable Gift

If while we were enemies we were reconciled to God by the death of his Son, much more, now that we are reconciled, shall we be saved by his life. More than that, we also rejoice in God through our Lord Jesus Christ, through whom we have now received reconciliation.

—Romans 5:10-11

How do we practically receive reconciliation and exult in God? One answer is that we do it through Jesus Christ. That means, at least in part, that we make the portrait of Jesus in the Bible—the work and the words of Jesus portrayed in the New Testament—the essential content of our exultation over God. Exultation without the content of Christ does not honor Christ.

In 2 Corinthians 4:4-6, Paul describes conversion in two ways. In verse 4, he says it is from seeing "the glory of Christ, who is the image of God." And in verse 6, he says it is from seeing "the glory of God in the face of Jesus Christ." You see the point: We have Christ, the image of God, and we have God in the face of Christ.

Practically, to exult in God is to exult in what you see and know of God in the portrait of Jesus Christ. And this comes to its fullest experience when the love of God is poured out in our hearts by the Holy Spirit, as Romans 5:5 says.

Here's the Christmas point: Not only did God purchase our reconciliation through the death of the

Lord Jesus Christ (Romans 5:10), and not only did God enable us to receive that reconciliation through the Lord Jesus Christ (Romans 5:11), but even now, we exult in God himself through our Lord Jesus Christ.

Jesus purchased our reconciliation. He enabled us to receive the reconciliation and open the gift. And Jesus himself shines forth from the wrapping—the indescribable gift—as God in the flesh and stirs up all our exultation in God.

Look to Jesus this Christmas. Receive the reconciliation that he bought. Don't put it on the shelf unopened. And don't open it and then make it a means to all your other pleasures. Open it and enjoy the gift himself. Exult in him. Make him your pleasure. Make him your treasure.

DECEMBER 24
The Son of God Appeared

Little children, let no one deceive you. Whoever practices righteousness is righteous, as he is righteous. Whoever makes a practice of sinning is of the devil, for the devil has been sinning from the beginning. The reason the Son of God appeared was to destroy the works of the devil.

—1 John 3:7-8

*W*hat are the "works of the devil" that Jesus came to destroy? The answer is clear from the context. First, verse 5 is a clear parallel: "You know that he appeared to take away sins." So the "works of the devil" that Jesus came to destroy are sins. The first part of verse 8 makes this more plain: "Whoever makes a practice of sinning is of the devil, for the devil has been sinning from the beginning." The issue in this context is habitual sin, not sickness or broken cars or messed up schedules. Jesus came into the world to help us stop sinning.

Let me put it alongside the truth of 1 John 2:1: "My little children, I am writing these things to you so that you may not sin." In other words, I am promoting the purpose of Christmas (3:8), the purpose of the Incarnation. Then he adds, "But if anyone does sin, we have an advocate with the Father, Jesus Christ the righteous. He is the propitiation for our sins, and not for ours only, but also for the sins of the whole world" (1 John 2:1-2).

This means that Jesus appeared in the world for two reasons. He came that we might not go on sinning; and he came to die so that there would be a pro-pitiation—a substitutionary sacrifice that takes away the wrath of God—when we do sin.

DECEMBER 25
Three Christmas Presents

Little children, let no one deceive you. Whoever practices righteousness is righteous, as he is righteous. Whoever makes a practice of sinning is of the devil, for the devil has been sinning from the beginning. The reason the Son of God appeared was to destroy the works of the devil.

—1 John 3:7-8

*P*onder this remarkable situation with me. If the Son of God came to help you stop sinning—to destroy the works of the devil—and if he also came to die so that, when you do sin, there is a propitiation, a removal of God's wrath, then what does this imply for your life? Three things, and they are wonderful blessings. Think of them as Christmas presents.

1. A Clear Purpose for Living

Jesus coming to destroy sin gives you a clear purpose for living. Negatively, it is stated this way: "I am writing these things to you *so that you may not sin*" (1 John 2:1). "The reason the Son of God appeared was to destroy the works of the devil" (1 John 3:8).

This is all summed up positively in 1 John 3:23: "This is his commandment, that we believe in the name of his Son Jesus Christ and love one another, just as he has commanded us." These two things are so closely connected for John that he calls them one commandment: believe Jesus and love others. That is your purpose. That is the sum of the Christian life. Trust Jesus, love people. This is the first gift Jesus offers: a purpose to live.

2. Hope That Our Failures Will Be Forgiven

Now consider the second implication of the twofold truth that Christ came to destroy our habits of sin and to forgive our sins: We make progress in overcoming our sin when we have hope that our failures will be forgiven. If you don't have hope that God will forgive your failures, then you will give up the moment you sin.

Many of you are pondering some changes in the new year because you have fallen into sinful patterns and want out. You want some new patterns of eating. New patterns for entertainment. New patterns of giving. New patterns of relating to your spouse. New patterns of family devotions. New patterns of sleep and exercise. New patterns of courage in witness. But you are struggling, wondering whether it's any use. Well, here's your second Christmas present: Christ not only came to destroy the works of the devil—our sinning—he also came to be an advocate for us when we fail in our fight.

But beware! If you turn the grace of God into license, and say, "Well, if I can fail, and it doesn't matter, then why bother fighting?"—if you say that, and mean it, and go on acting on it, you are probably not born again and should tremble.

But that is not where most of you are. Most of you want to fight sinful patterns in your life. And what God is saying to you is this: Let the freedom to fail give you hope to fight. I write this to you that you might not sin, but if you sin you have an advocate, Jesus Christ.

3. Supernatural Help in the Fight against Sin

Finally, the third implication of the double truth that Christ came to destroy our habits of sin and to forgive our sins is this: Christ will really help us in our fight. He is on our side. He didn't come to destroy sin because sin is fun, he came to destroy sin because it is fatal. It is a deceptive work of the devil and will destroy us if we don't fight it. He came to help us, not hurt us.

So here's your third Christmas gift: Christ will help overcome sin in you. First John 4:4 says, "He who is in you is greater than he who is in the world." Jesus is alive, Jesus is almighty, Jesus lives in us by faith. And Jesus is for you, not against you. He will help you. Trust him.

CONCLUSION
My Favorite Christmas Text

This Christmas I am marveling at Jesus' humility and wanting more of it myself. In fact, my favorite Christmas text centers on humility.

Now, there are two problems with focusing on humility. Tim Keller helps us to see one of them when he says, "Humility is shy. If you begin talking about it, it leaves." A meditation on humility (like this one) is somewhat self-defeating, it seems. But even shy people peek out sometimes if they are treated well.

The other problem is that Jesus wasn't humble for the same reasons we are (or should be). So how can looking at Jesus' Christmas humility help us? Our humility, if there is any at all, is based on our finiteness, fallibility, and sinfulness. But the eternal Son of God was not finite. He was not fallible. And he was not sinful. Yet he was humble.

> *Though he was in the form of God, [Jesus] did not count equality with God a thing to be grasped, but made himself nothing, taking the form of a servant, being born in the likeness of men. And being found in human form, he humbled himself by becoming obedient to the point of death, even death on a cross.*
>
> —Philippians 2:6-8

Jesus' humility was a conscious act of putting himself in a lowly, servant role for the good of others. His humility is defined by phrases like:

› "he made himself nothing" [emptying himself of his divine rights to be free from abuse and suffering].

› "he took the form of a servant."

› "he became obedient to the point of death, even death on a cross."

Jesus' humility did not arise from being finite or fallible or sinful. His heart is infinite perfection and infallible truthfulness and freedom from all sin, and for that very reason he did not need to be served. He was free and full to overflow in serving.

Consider Mark 10:45: "The Son of Man came not to be served but to serve, and to give his life as a ransom for many." Jesus' humility did not arise from any sense of defect in himself, but from a sense of fullness in himself put at the disposal of others for their good. It was a voluntary lowering of himself to make the height of his glory available for sinners to enjoy. Jesus makes the connection between his lowliness and the good news for us: "Come to me, all who labor and are heavy laden, and I will give you rest. Take my yoke upon you, and learn from me, for I am gentle and lowly in heart, and you will find rest for your souls. For my yoke is easy, and my burden is light" (Matthew 11:28-30).

His lowliness makes possible relief from our burdens. If he were not lowly, he would not have been "obedient unto death, even death on a cross." And if he had not been obedient to die for us, we would be crushed under the weight of our sins. He lowered himself to take our condemnation (Romans 8:3).

Now we have more reason to be humble than ever before. We are finite, fallible, sinful, and therefore have no ground for boasting at all. Our salvation is not owing to our work, but his grace. So boasting is excluded (Ephesians 2:8-9). And the way Jesus accomplished our gracious salvation was through voluntary, conscious self-lowering in servant-like obedience to the point of death.

So in addition to finiteness, fallibility, and sinfulness, we now have two other huge impulses at work to humble us: free and undeserved grace underneath all our blessings and a model of self-denying, sacrificial, servanthood that willingly takes the form of a servant. We are called to join Jesus in this conscious self-humbling and servanthood. "Whoever exalts himself will be humbled, and whoever humbles himself will be exalted" (Matthew 23:12). "Have this mind among yourselves, which is yours in Christ Jesus . . ." (Philippians 2:5).

Let's pray that this "shy virtue"—this massive ground of our salvation and our servanthood—would peek out from her quiet place and grant us the garments of lowliness this Advent. "Clothe yourselves, all of you, with humility toward one another, for 'God opposes the proud but gives grace to the humble'" (1 Peter 5:5).

APPENDIX

Old Testament Shadows and the Coming of Christ

One of the main points of the book of Hebrews is that the old covenant system of worship is a shadow replaced by Christ. Christmas is the replacement of shadows with reality. (You can see this in Hebrews 8:5, where it says that the priests "serve a copy and shadow of the heavenly things.")

Consider six shadows that the coming of Christ replaces with reality.

1. **The shadow of the old covenant priesthood.** "The former priests were many in number, because they were prevented by death from continuing in office, but he holds his priesthood permanently, because he continues forever" (Hebrews 7:23-24).

2. **The shadow of the Passover sacrifice.** "Cleanse out the old leaven that you may be a new lump, as you really are unleavened. For Christ, our Passover lamb, has been sacrificed" (1 Corinthians 5:7).

3. **The shadow of the Tabernacle and Temple.** "Now the point in what we are saying is this: we have such a high priest, one who is seated at the right hand of the throne of the Majesty in heaven, a minister in the holy places, in the true tent that the Lord set up, not man" (Hebrews 8:1-2).

"Jesus answered them, 'Destroy this temple, and in three days I will raise it up.' The Jews then said, 'It has taken forty-six years to build this temple, and will you raise it up in three days?' But he was speaking about the temple of his body" (John 2:19-21).

4. **The shadow of circumcision.** "Neither circumcision counts for anything nor uncircumcision, but keeping the commandments of God" (1 Corinthians 7:19).

5. **The shadow of dietary laws.** "And he said to them, 'Then are you also without understanding? Do you not see that whatever goes into a person from outside cannot defile him, since it enters not his heart but his stomach, and is expelled?' (Thus he declared all foods clean.)" (Mark 7:18-19).

6. **The shadow of feast days.** "Therefore let no one pass judgment on you in questions of food and drink, or with regard to a festival or a new moon or a Sabbath. These are a shadow of is the things to come, but the substance belongs to Christ" (Colossians 2:16-17).

That, in a nutshell, is the meaning of Christmas: the substance belongs to Christ. Religious ritual is like a shadow of a great and glorious Person. Let us turn from the shadow and look the Person in the face (2 Corinthians 4:6).

The mission of Desiring God is that people everywhere would understand and embrace the truth that God is most glorified in us when we are most satisfied in him. Our primary strategy for accomplishing this mission is through a maximally useful website that houses over thirty years of John Piper's preaching and teaching, including translations into more than 40 languages. This is all available free of charge, thanks to our generous ministry partners. If you would like to further explore the vision of Desiring God, we encourage you to visit www.desiringGod.org.

Desiring God

Post Office Box 2901, Minneapolis, Minnesota 55402
888.346.4700 mail@desiringGod.org